Exercises and Etudes for the
JAZZ INSTRUMENTALIST

TREBLE CLEF EDITION

by J.J. Johnson

ISBN 0-634-02865-0

7777 W. Bluemound Rd. P.O. Box 13819 Milwaukee, WI 53213

Visit Hal Leonard Online at
www.halleonard.com

A Jazz Etude

Dedication

I would very much like to dedicate this method book to the memory of Fred Lee Beckett, a very gifted jazz trombonist and one of several major influences early on in my career. He died in 1945 at the age of 28 years old. He was never well-known, which is all the more reason that I wish to make this dedication.

His style of trombone jazz improvisation was very melodic, which left a lasting impression on me. He appeared as featured trombone soloist with The Harlan Leonard Rockets on some few recordings that were once available. My favorite trombone solo of his was on the Harlan Leonard Rockets' recording of "My Gal Sal." Other solos were on "Skee" and "Ala Bridges." I will always regret the fact that I never met him in person, and never heard him perform live. Nevertheless, it gives me great pleasure to dedicate this method book to the memory of Fred Lee Beckett.

J.J. Johnson

Foreword

This method book is based primarily on my own personal experiences and career as a jazz trombonist, and therefore has very little to do with dogma or tenets. This book is not intended as an alternative or replacement for the many excellent trombone method books that are available to you. It is intended as an extension of these books. It is my sincere hope that this book will make a small but meaningful contribution towards removing some of the mysterious aura of jazz improvisation since jazz improvisation is the core element in jazz music. Removing that rampant and arcane mystery is a very tough challenge, but I am committed towards having a shot at it. In my opinion, if jazz improvisation is the heart and soul of jazz music, then a clear and basic understanding of jazz syntax (or the language of jazz) is the necessary heart and soul of jazz improvisation. With this book I am committed to helping you get a basic and clear understanding of jazz syntax.

Part One will be somewhat familiar to most of you.

Part Two deals head on with jazz syntax by way of original melodies that I choose to call Jazz Etudes, composed for unaccompanied solo trombone by yours truly. There will be no chord symbols, or other extraneous items to distract us from the pursuit of melodic or linear thinking, in our quest to make jazz syntax more user-friendly.

I have carefully examined the etude books by Rochut, Bordogni, as well as others. They all deserve to be as highly regarded as they are.

And now, to get the show on the road,

Let us begin with some entry level melodic exercises. The advanced players may elect to skip over this section, and move on to long lones (page 26), scales, etc., or move straight-away into Part Two (page 44). Depending on your instrument, you may need to play these pieces an octave higher.

Hopefully, your curiosity will not allow you to skip over anything if you are still learning the fundamentals.

In Part One, after the entry level melodic exercises, we will revisit areas that are somewhat familiar to most of you, as I mentioned before — long tones, scale patterns, cyclical patterns, etc.

And now, let us move forward to the Melodic Exercises, posthaste.

Part One

Melodic Exercises

Melodic Exercise 2

Melodic Exercise 3

Melodic Exercise 4

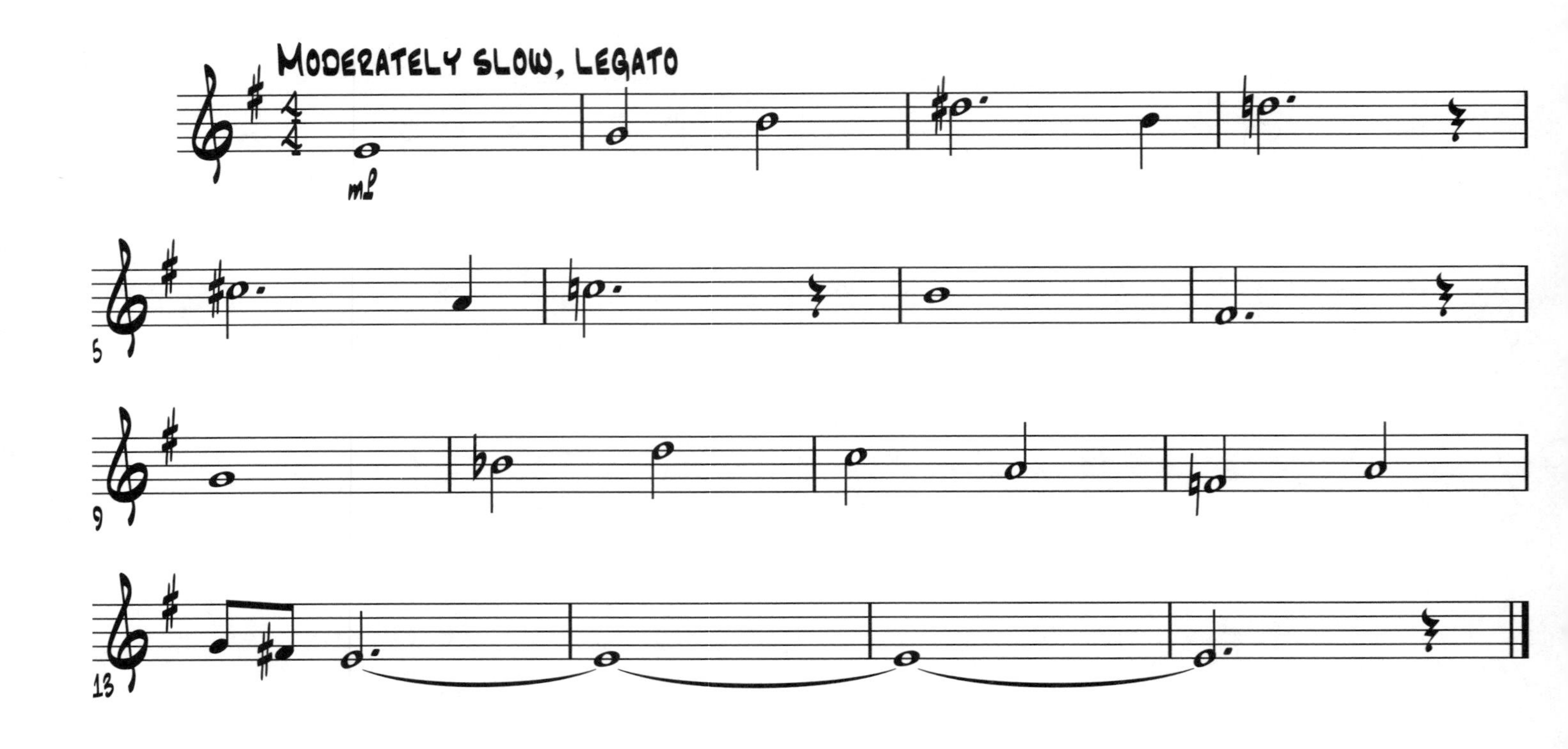

Melodic Exercise 5

Melodic Exercise 6

Melodic Exercise 7

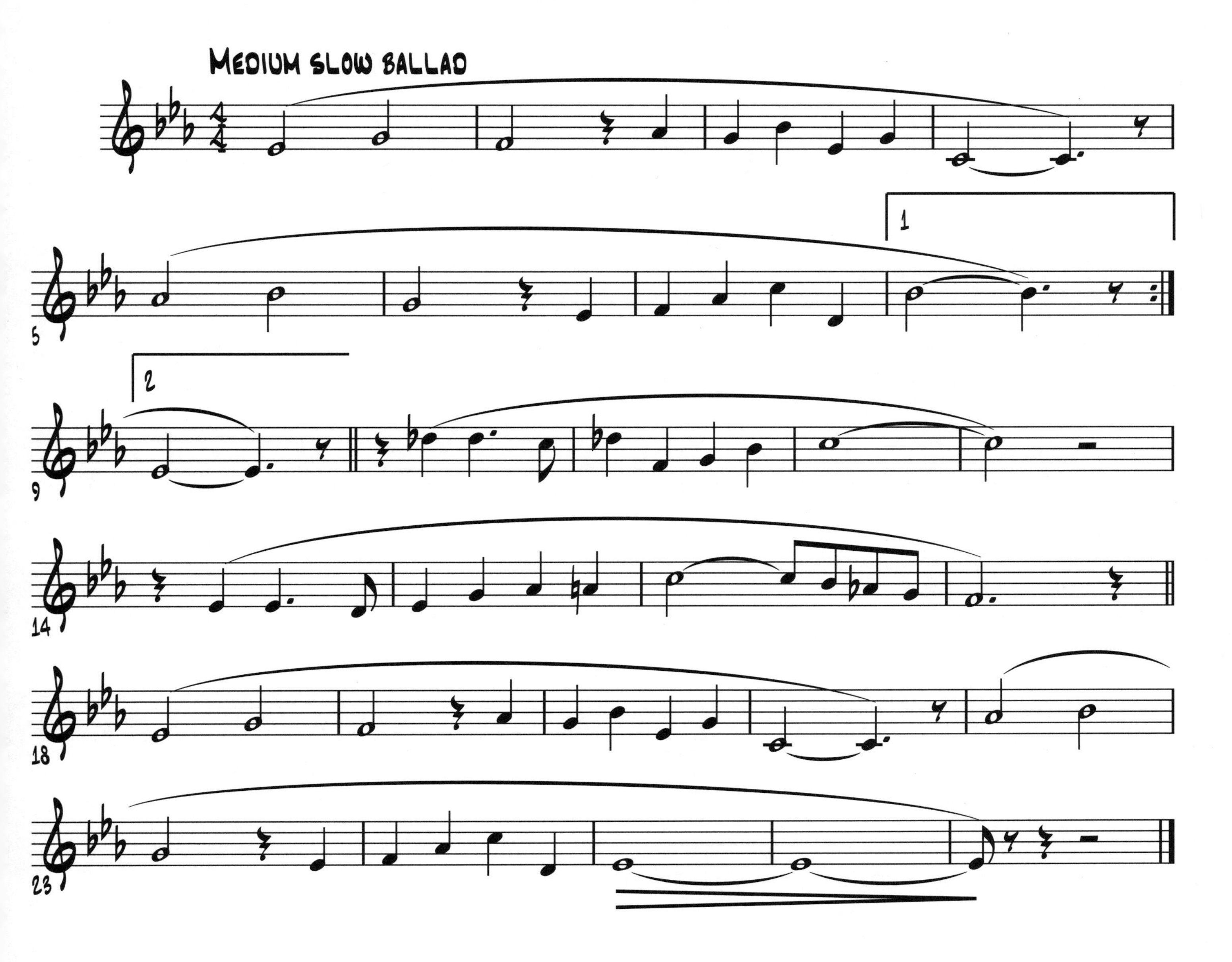

Melodic Exercise 8

Melodic Exercise 9

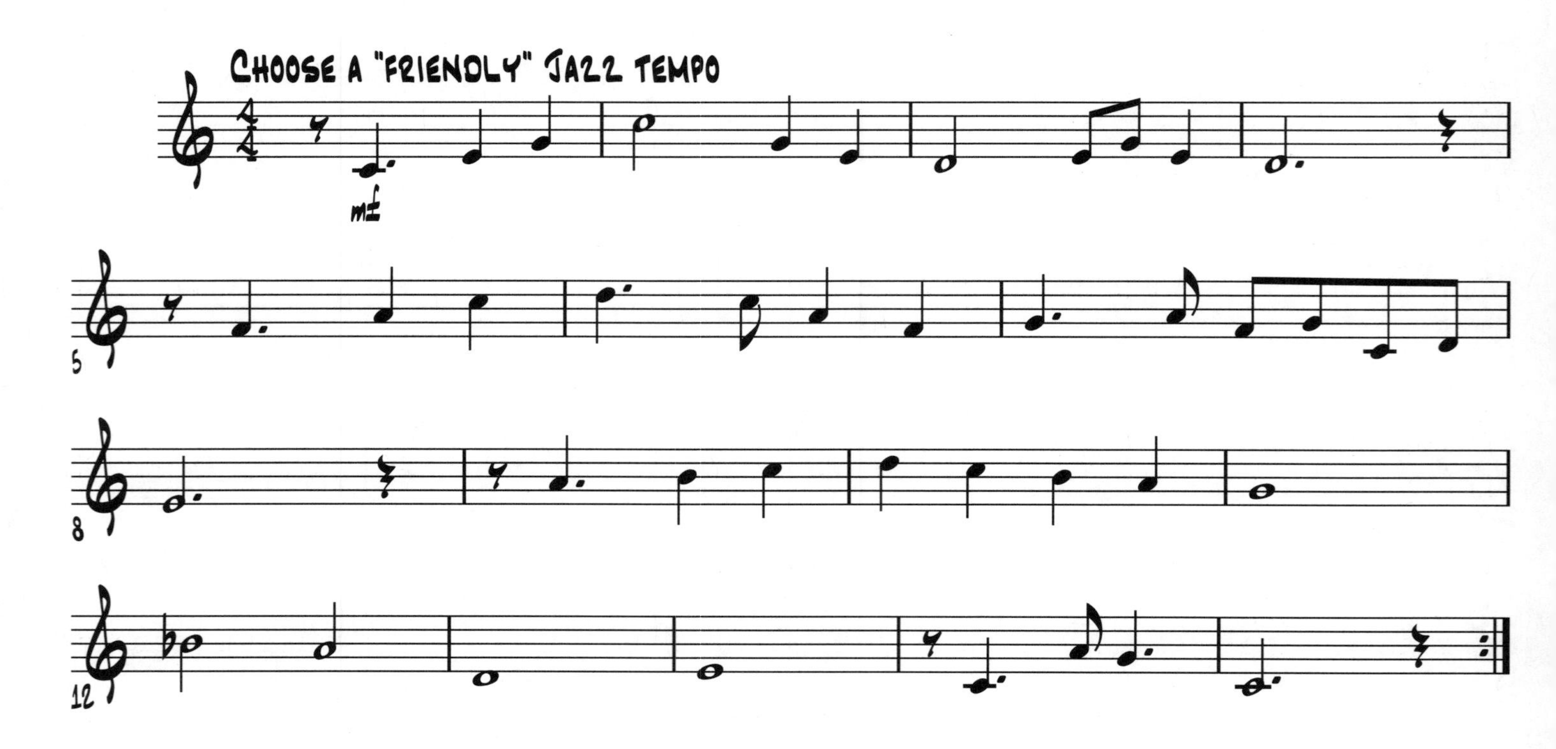

Melodic Exercise 10

Melodic Exercise 11

Entr'acte

And why not?

Melodic Exercise 12

Melodic Exercise 13

Melodic Exercise 14

Melodic Exercise 15

13
17
23
29
33
37
41
45

MELODIC EXERCISE 16

Melodic Exercise 17

Melodic Exercise 18

Melodic Exercise 19

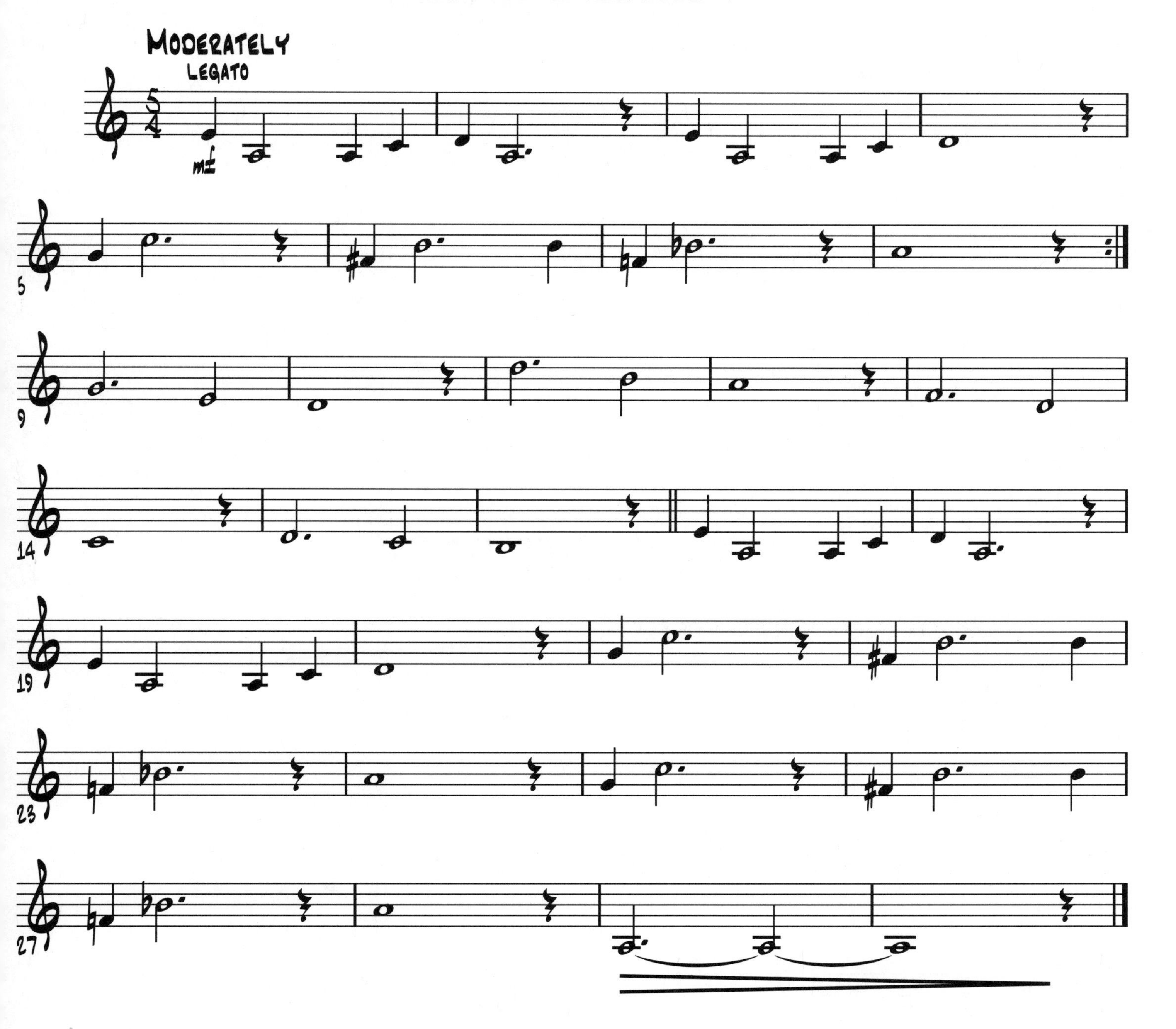

Melodic Exercise 20

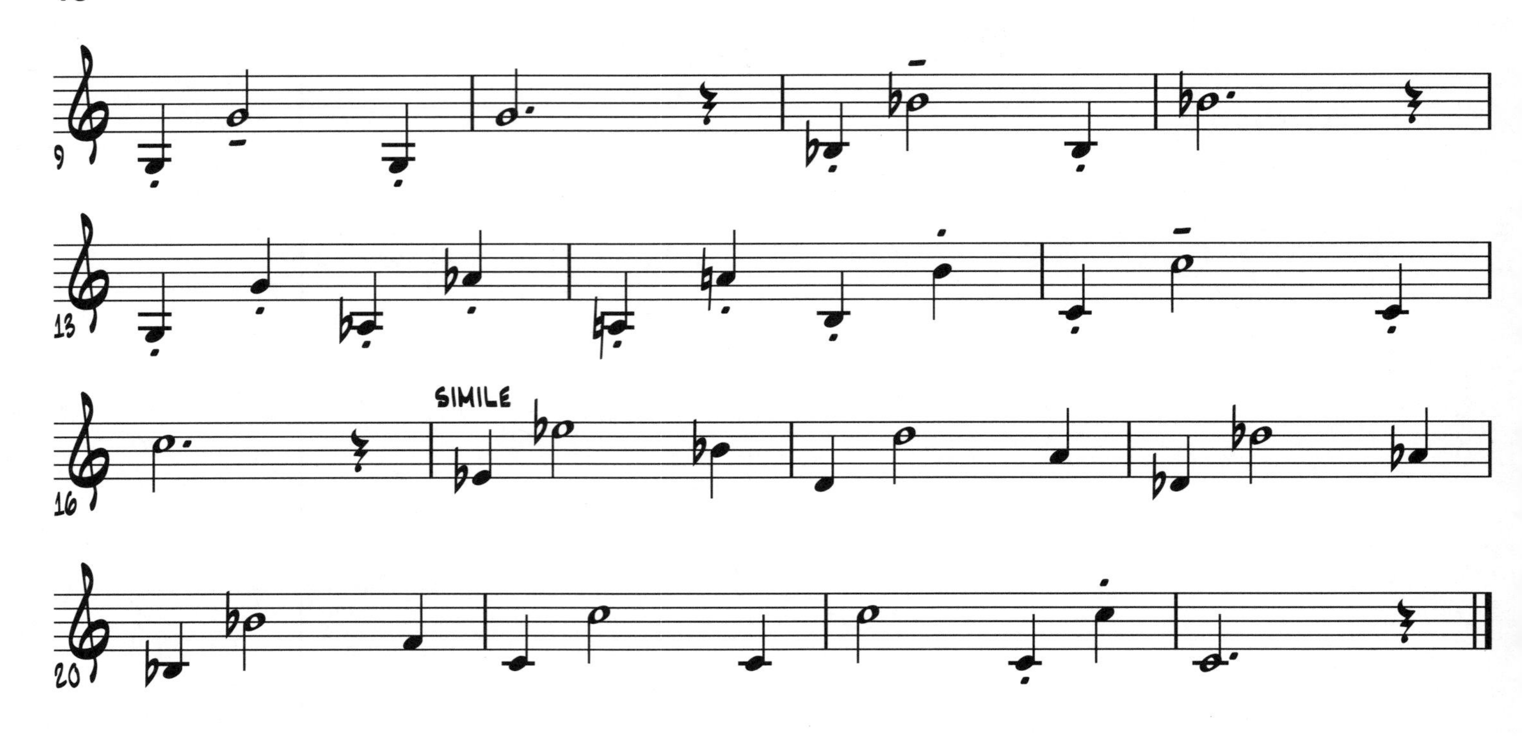

MELODIC EXERCISE 21

MELODIC EXERCISE 22

MELODIC EXERCISE 23

Melodic Exercise 24

MELODIC EXERCISE 25

Melodic Exercise 26

25
29
33
37
40
43
47
ff

THE FAT LADY

Encore

But, of course.

LONG TONES, A DIFFERENT APPROACH

WE ARE ON A ROLL, CAN YOU FEEL IT?

So much for linear long tones. And now we will begin to get into the area of our objective, which of course has to do with linear thinking, in general.

We will begin by just moving around a bit on the trombone.

The degree of difficulty may increase as we move around.

Any tempo, breathe anywhere, sustain anywhere, Stop anywhere, articulate as you like.

What is important is the melodic/harmonic content.

START TO MOVE AROUND

Ditto, as previous "Start to Move Around."

MORE MOVE AROUND

9/8 CAPER

Any tempo, breathe anywhere, sustain anywhere, stop anywhere.

NOT FOR EVERYONE?

WHO SEZ?

(NOT FOR EVERYONE)

13

15

17

19

21

23
pp

II, V, I CHORDS – CYCLICAL

BRISK

5/4

9th Chord

TRIADS

Mixed Chords

3
3

COFFEE BREAK

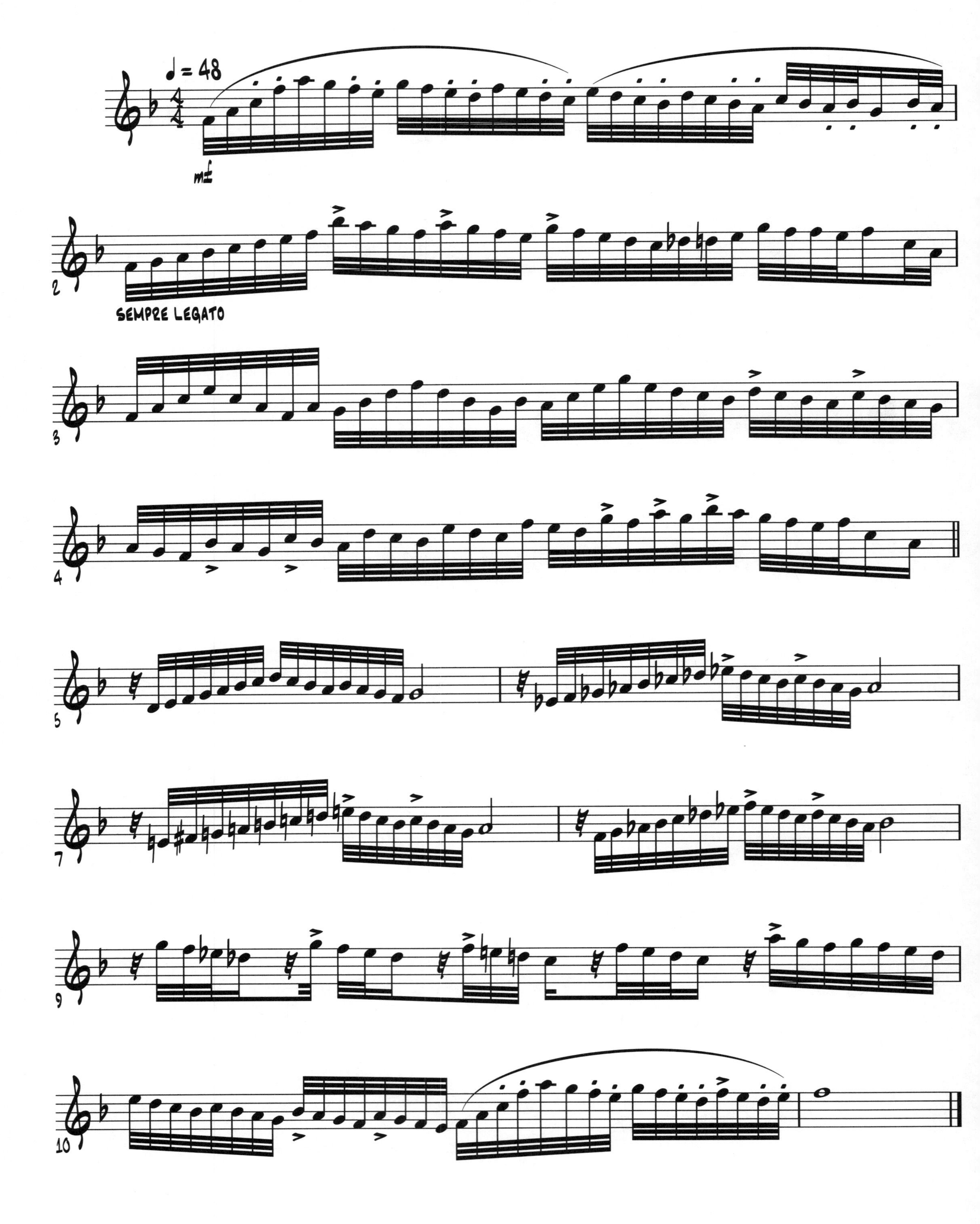

OCTAVE PLUS – JUMPS

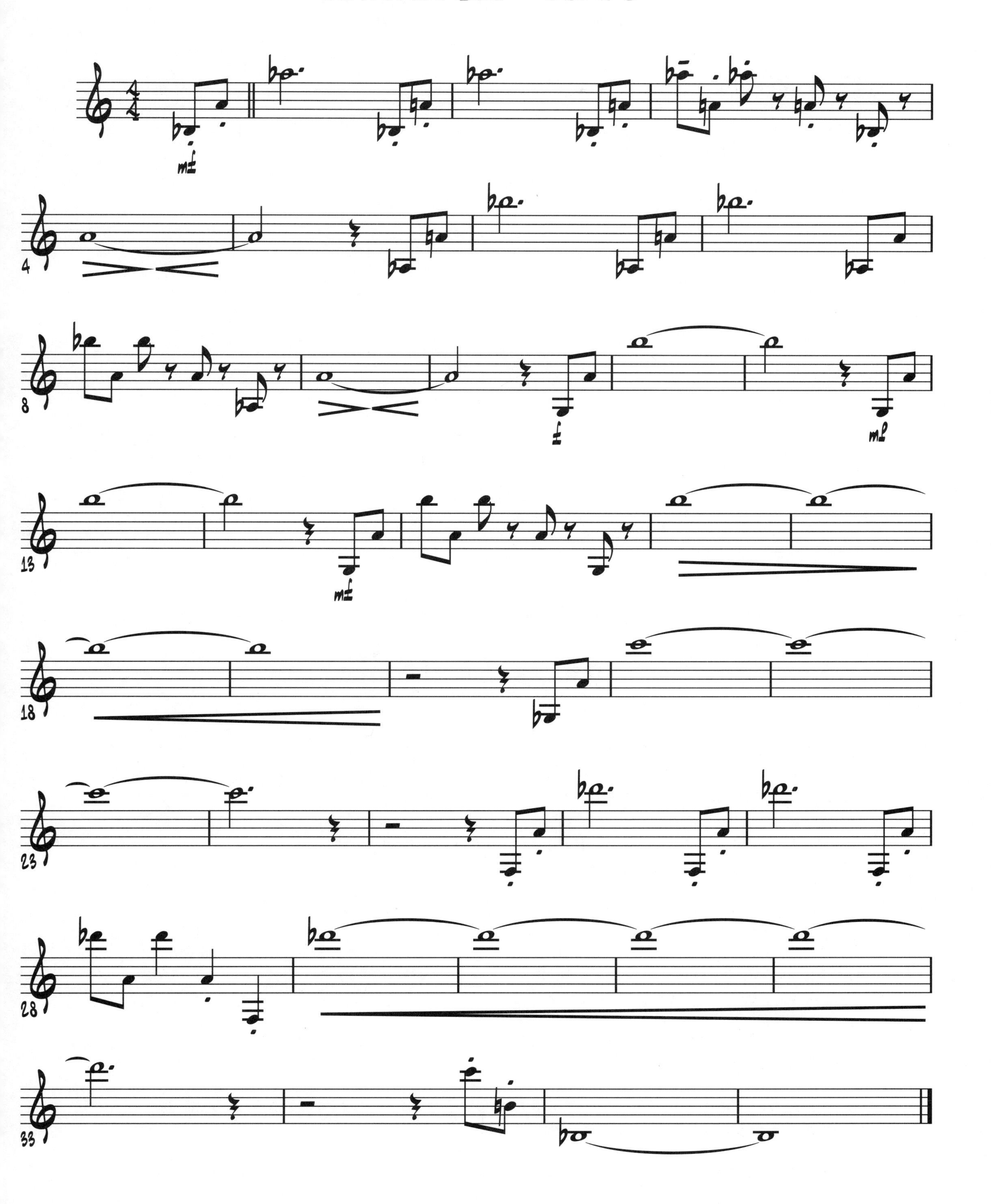

With Octave Plus – Jumps we come to the end of Part One of this Method book.

I thought that it went rather well. ;)

The Burning Question:

How did you feel about it ? ?

In any case, Part Two awaits your pleasure and indulgence.

Part Two

JAZZ ETUDES

JAZZ, THE NAUGHTY CHILD (AND JAZZ 8TH NOTES)

Jazz music is fraught (and blessed) with certain ambiguities. One of the many reasons for this is that jazz, like the proverbial naughty child that it is, is always "getting into something" that it shouldn't get into. (This is one of the reasons why we love it so much.)

It got into trouble when it met up with pop music. It got into trouble when it met up with rock & roll. It got into trouble recently when it met up with rap (music?).

That is why jazz music as we know it today is so splintered, and so hybrid-ized. Some of you may even think that it is a good thing, these jazz hybrids. Don't get me wrong: I too like some of the hybrid stuff that I hear, and especially jazz fusion. I too own MIDI gear, synthesizers and other computer peripherals that go into the composing of jazz fusion music. Some of the so-called "cross-over" jazz is very interesting and very exciting, for sure.

But I can never ever forget the fact that I am a bona fide jazz purist. At the considerable risk of sounding "Holier than thou," I really prefer the "Dizzy, Bird, Miles, Coltrane, Monk, etc." brand of jazz music.

That brings me full circle to another area of ambiguity in jazz music, and that is the controversial subject of jazz 8th notes, and jazz feel.

As regards 8th-note articulation, what is jazz feel?

Jazz 8th notes are a cross between:

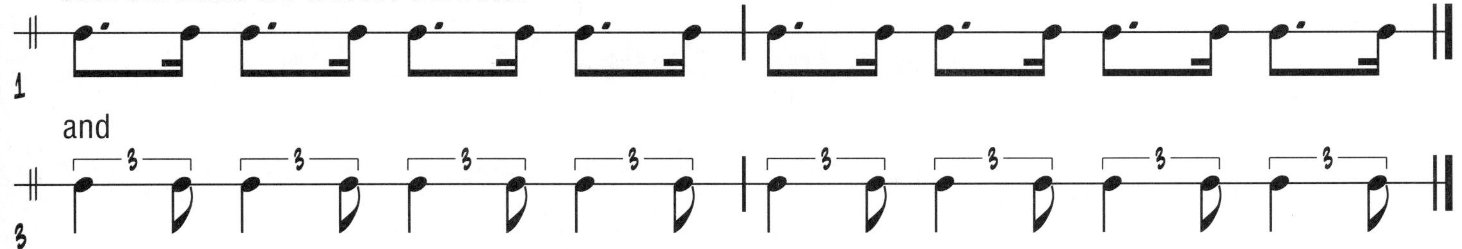

INTERBREEDING ?

One has to wonder about the "in between-ness" of the situation. In my opinion, somewhere along the road of the evolution of jazz syntax, it just happened. To get a better grip on the situation, I would urge you to listen to the vintage recordings of Louis Armstrong, especially his classic version of "Basin Street Blues."

Also, listen to vintage recordings of trombonists Jack Teagarden and Bill Harris, and Count Basie tenor saxophone soloist Lester Young (my first jazz improv hero, when I was in high school.)

Other than that, not to worry.

Jazz 8th notes and jazz feel will at some point just come to you naturally and with a minimum of effort.

While playing the Jazz Etudes, you will also encounter, on some occasions, the term "Laid Back." What does this mean?

The tempo indication "Laid Back" is intended to be an attitude (mind games?) more than anything else. Much of rock & roll music, funk music, jazz fusion music, and even gospel music is laid back in style and attitude. That is a good thing and a fun thing. For me, it means to relax, think just a tiny bit behind the beat without actually playing behind the beat, and sometimes add a touch of earthiness to your playing style. Experimentation will bring about the desired result. You will see.

I know, I know, you want to get to the music. OK, OK. So do I. I only have this final situation to bring to your attention. Please carefully compare A and B styles of music notation.

In this jazz method book, I will notate mostly in the B style, which is the norm for the most part. However, on occasion, I will use the A style to keep us awake–on our toes, and to keep things interesting.

Very Important Info

Jazz Etudes #1 through #35 are

ENTRY LEVEL ETUDES.

From #36 to the end of the Etudes, you are on your own.

JAZZ ETUDE 1

JAZZ ETUDE 2

JAZZ ETUDE 3

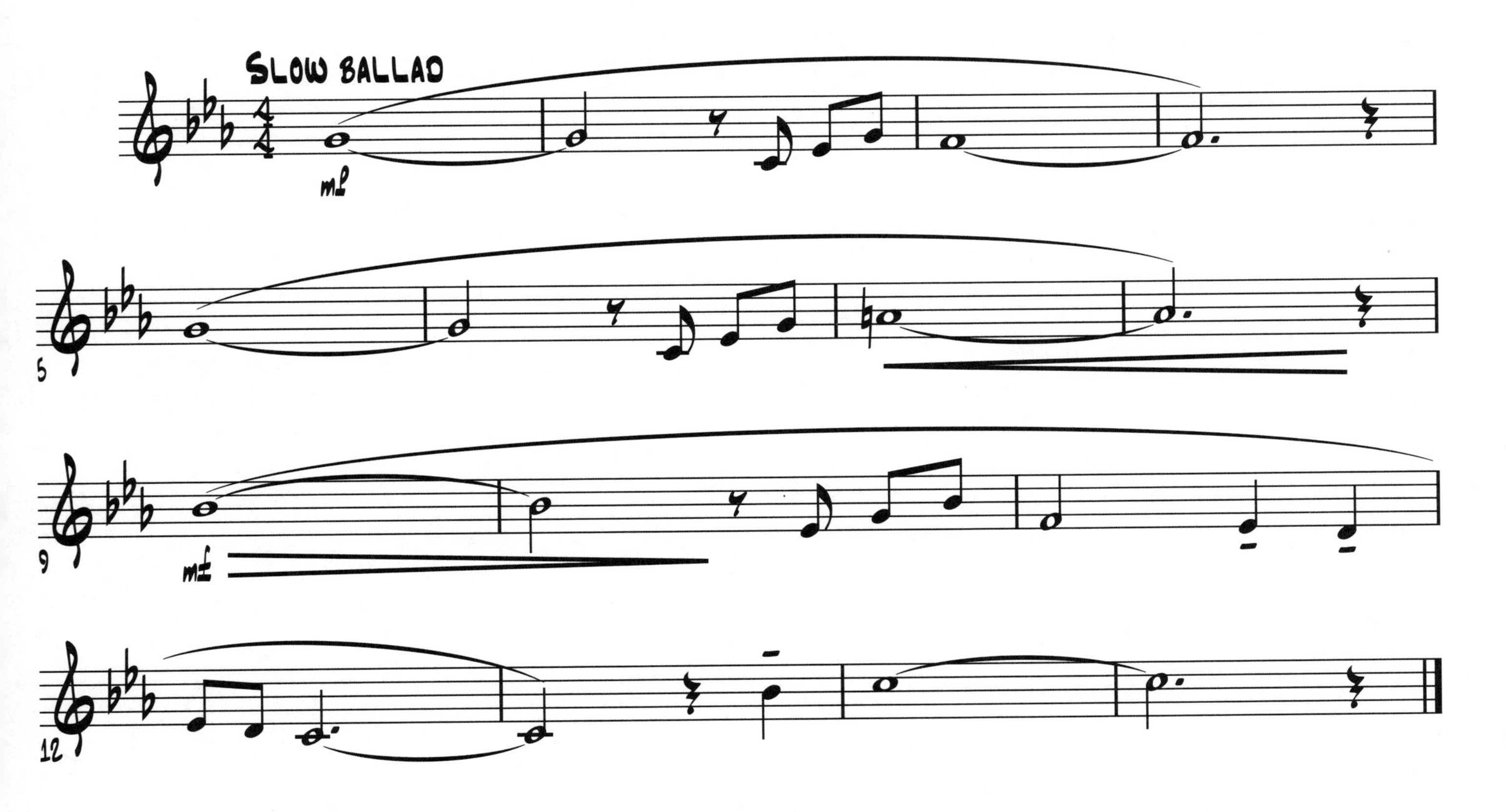

JAZZ ETUDE 4

56
mf
61
66
71
76
81
86
91
96
101
106
ff

JAZZ ETUDE 5

JAZZ ETUDE 6

mf
f
mf
pp
f

JAZZ ETUDE 7

MEDIUM SLOW BALLAD (EVEN EIGHTHS)
mf
SEMPRE LEGATO
RIT.

JAZZ ETUDE 8

JAZZ ETUDE 9

JAZZ ETUDE 10

pp
mf
mf
mf
f
pp
mf

How do you feel? Don't overdue it.
When your body is trying to tell you something,
LISTEN ! ! ! AND OBEY ! ! !

JAZZ ETUDE 11

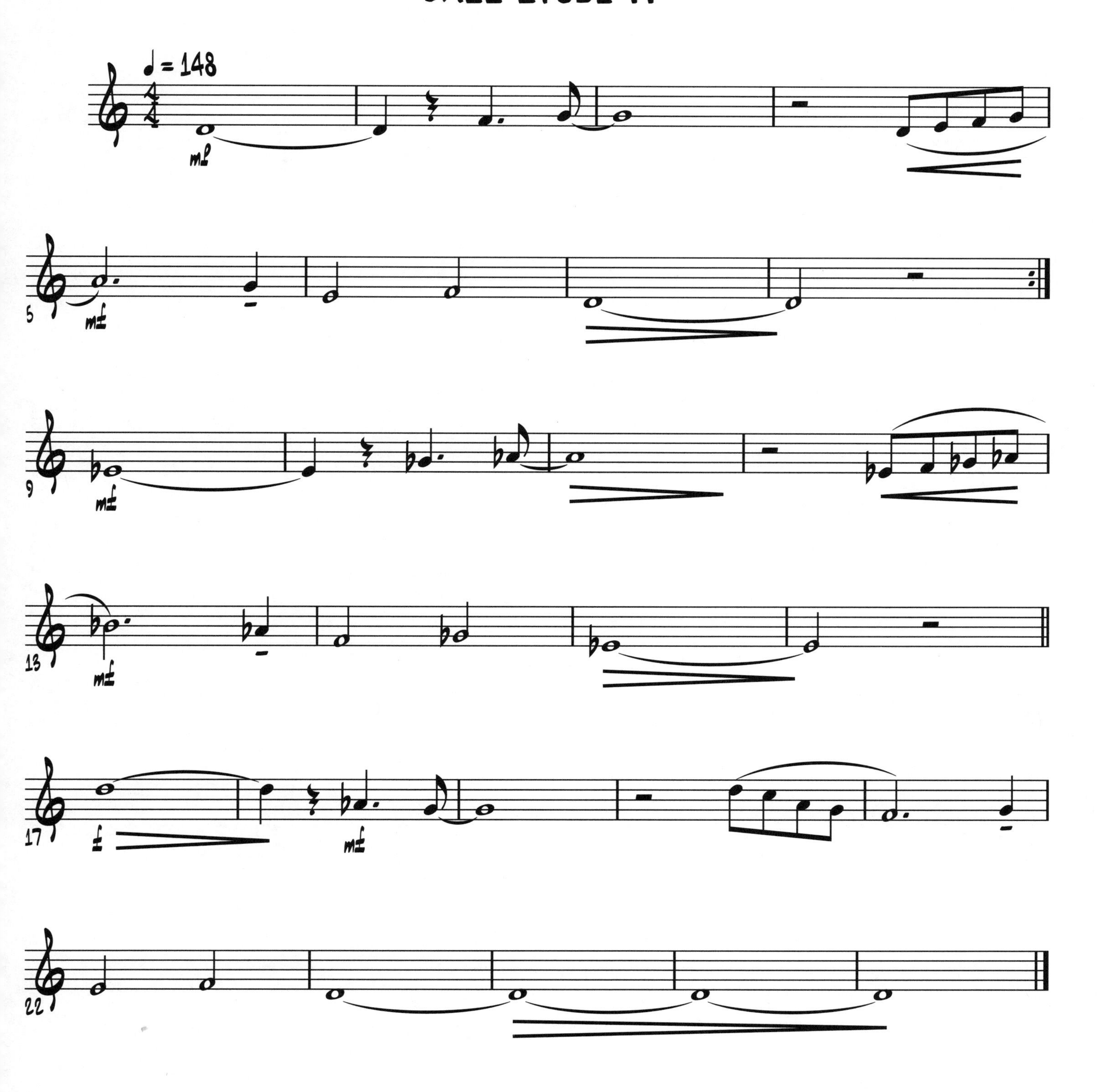

Jazz Etude 12

JAZZ ETUDE 13

JAZZ ETUDE 14

JAZZ ETUDE 15

JAZZ ETUDE 16

JAZZ ETUDE 17

Jazz Etude 18

21
mf

25

29

33

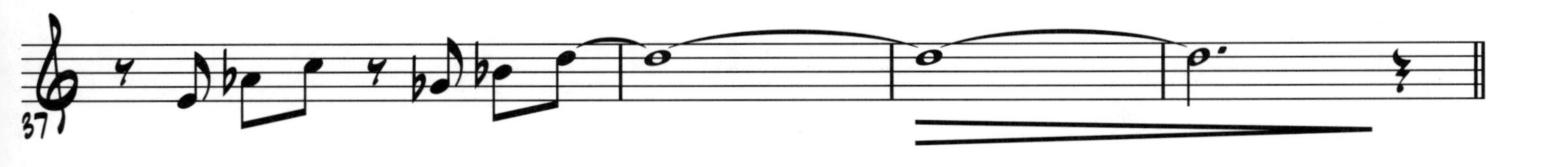
37

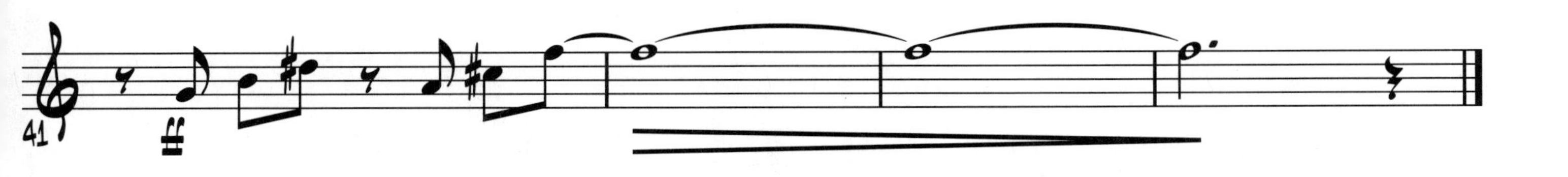
41
ff

JAZZ ETUDE 19

13
17
19
21
23
26

JAZZ ETUDE 20

SIM.

JAZZ ETUDE 21

JAZZ ETUDE 22

How do you feel? Don't overdue it.

When your body is trying to tell you something,

LISTEN ! ! !   AND OBEY ! ! !

JAZZ ETUDE 23

JAZZ ETUDE 24

JAZZ ETUDE 25

Jazz Etude 26

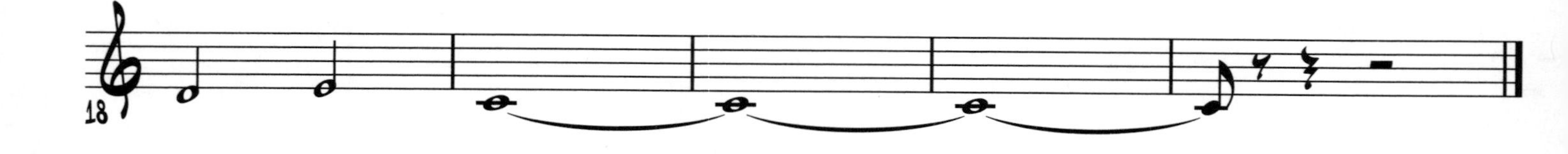

Jazz Etude 27

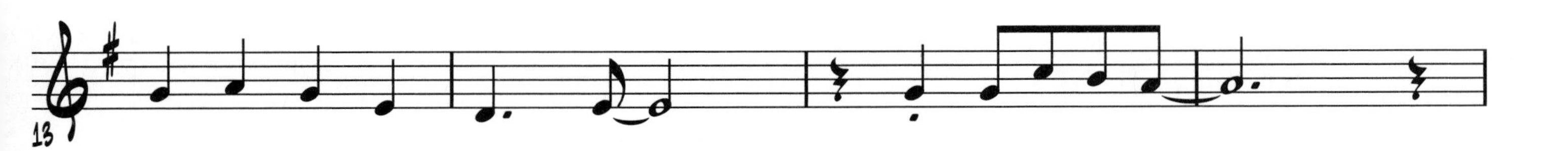

JAZZ ETUDE 28

JAZZ ETUDE 29

JAZZ ETUDE 30

JAZZ ETUDE 31

JAZZ ETUDE 32

JAZZ ETUDE 33

Jazz Etude 34

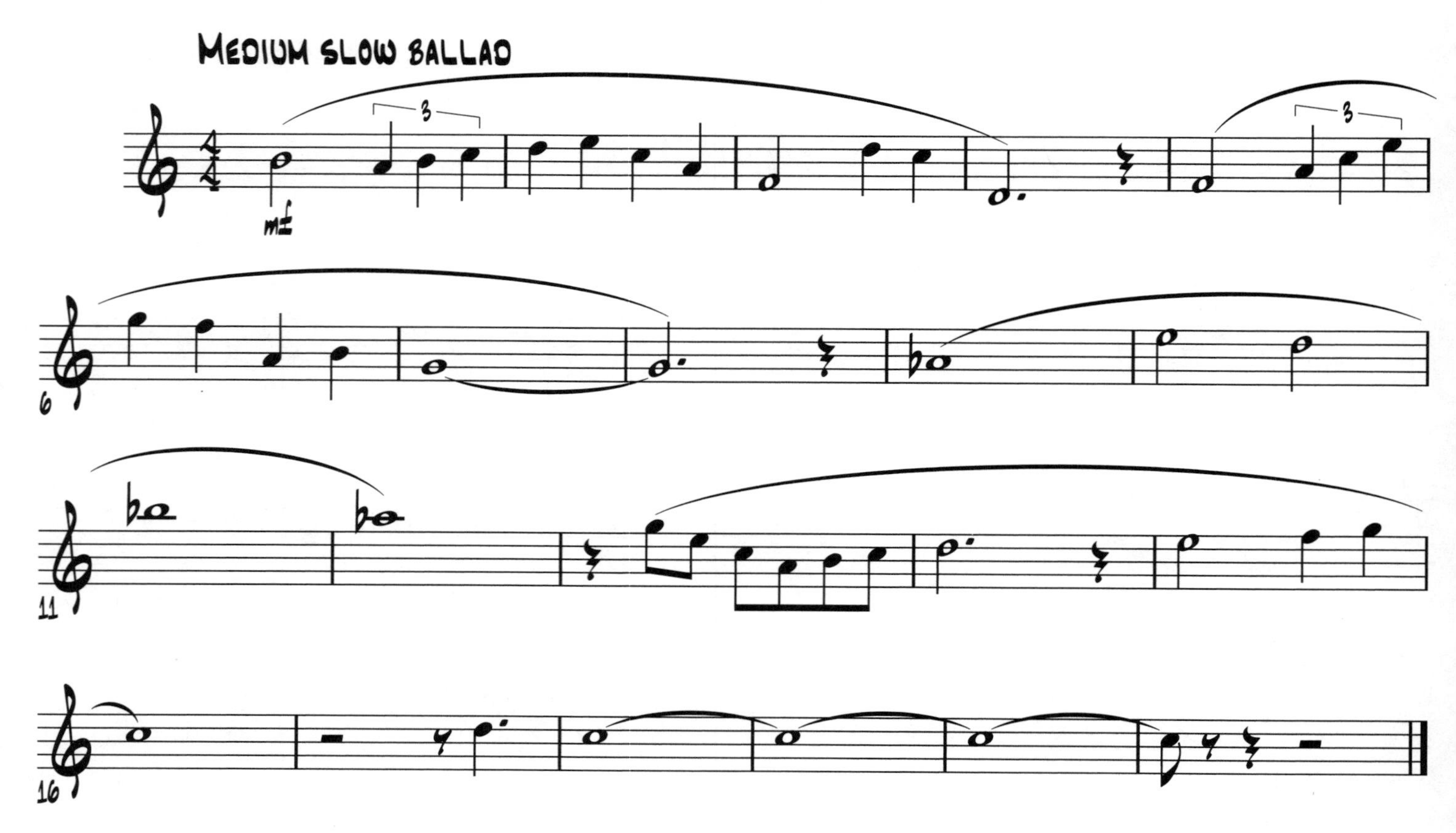

Jazz Etude 35
(Final Entry Level Etude)

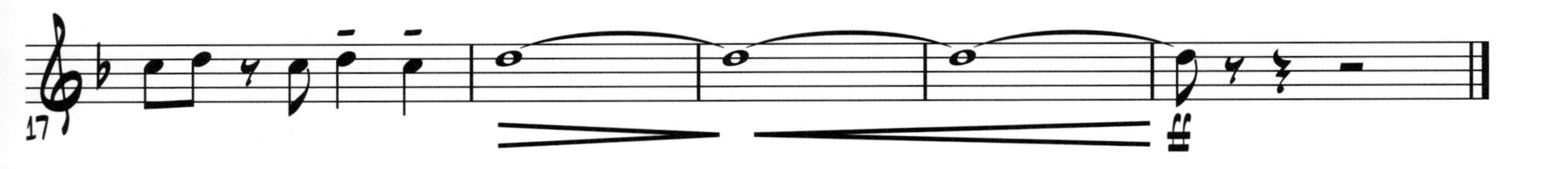

JAZZ ETUDE 36

(JAZZ-BLUES)

Jazz Etude 37

This etude is a tribute to my dear friend, Al Grey, who passed March 24, 2000. He was truly a remarkable trombonist and a plunger genius.

Jazz Etude 38

JAZZ ETUDE 39

JAZZ ETUDE 40
(OCTAVE BLUES)

JAZZ ETUDE 41

12
16
20
24
28
32
36
40
43

JAZZ ETUDE 42

JAZZ ETUDE 43

41
mf
44
SIM.
47
50
53
56
59
62
65
70
75
fff

JAZZ ETUDE 44
(CRAZY)

JAZZ ETUDE 45

BLUES, FAST, SNAPPY ♩ = 120

JAZZ ETUDE 46

This advise is from personal experience: If you're a brass player, keep a spare mouthpiece in the glove compartment of your car. Instead of talking so much on the cell phone, why not buzz on the mouthpiece while waiting for the red light to turn green? I also keep a spare mouthpiece next to my computer, and still another spare mouthpiece on the window ledge in my bathroom. :-)

(The habit mentioned above is in ADDITION to regular practice, NOT INSTEAD of practice.)

Jazz Etude 47

33
mf
36
pp
40
mf
43
3
46
mf
49
52
56
pp
f
60
mf

JAZZ ETUDE 48

Additional Info on Phrasing, in General

You will find that some of the etudes are very meticulously marked as regards phrasing. Others are marked minimally. There is a reason for this:

Yes, phrasing marks and indications are important, in general, and can give character to a musical statement. That truism notwithstanding, there are situations where less is more, especially in jazz music. Also, I hoped that on some etudes YOU would add phrasing as YOU saw fit. Even phrasing can be improvised, and it can be both challenging and enjoyable.

The bottom line is: MELODY REIGNS SUPREME ! ! !

This is true not only in jazz music, but in most musical genres. So stay loose and relaxed about phrasing.

Jazz Etude 49

So you say it's not Jazz? Sez' who? Maybe yes, maybe no.
Hmmmmmmmmmmm :-)

JAZZ ETUDE 50

p
CRESC.
p
CRESC.

Jazz Etude 51

(A Bit of Quasi Funk)

And why not?

Jazz Etude 52
(Fast Track)

mf

JAZZ ETUDE 53

JAZZ ETUDE 54

39
ppp cresc.
43
47
fff
mf
51
55
59
63
p
67
71
fff

JAZZ ETUDE 55

JAZZ ETUDE 56

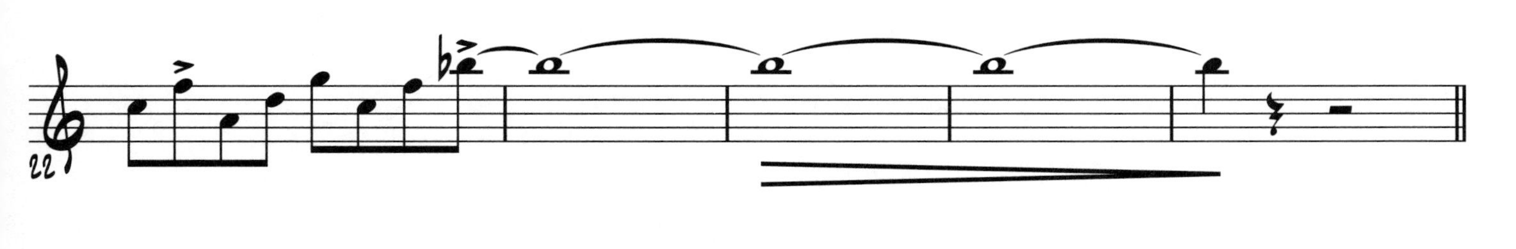
22

27
mf

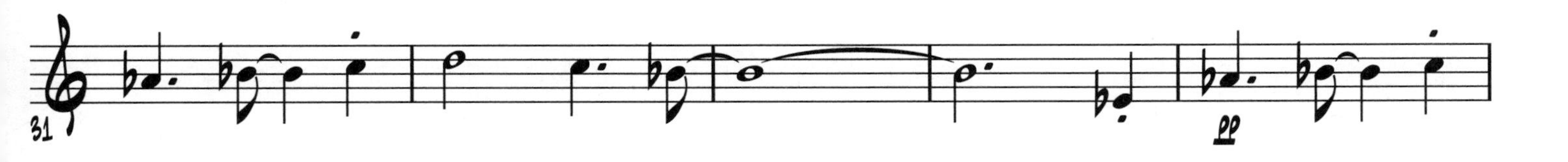
31
pp

36
f

40
mf
mf

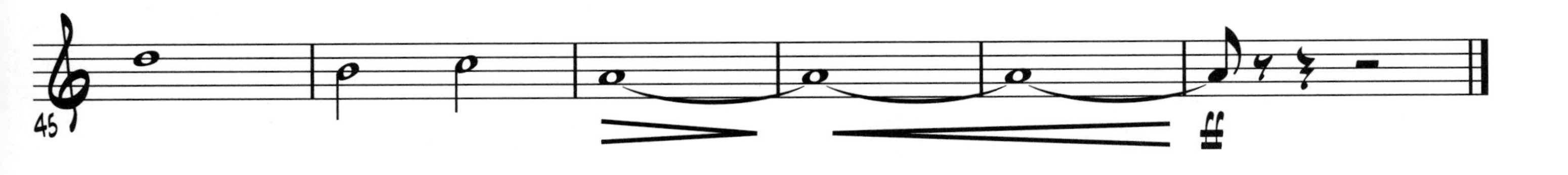
45
ff

Jazz Etude 57

JAZZ ETUDE 58

JAZZ ETUDE 59

JAZZ ETUDE 60

22
25
28
31
34
38
41
44

JAZZ ETUDE 61

mf

59
61
65
68
72
75
78
82
88
p
f
mf

Jazz Etude 62

♩ = 160
25
29
33
36
40
43
46
49
52
55

58
61
65
68
73
3
76
(♮)
80
3
3
83
87
90

93
97
100
103
106
109
112
115
118
121

JAZZ ETUDE 63

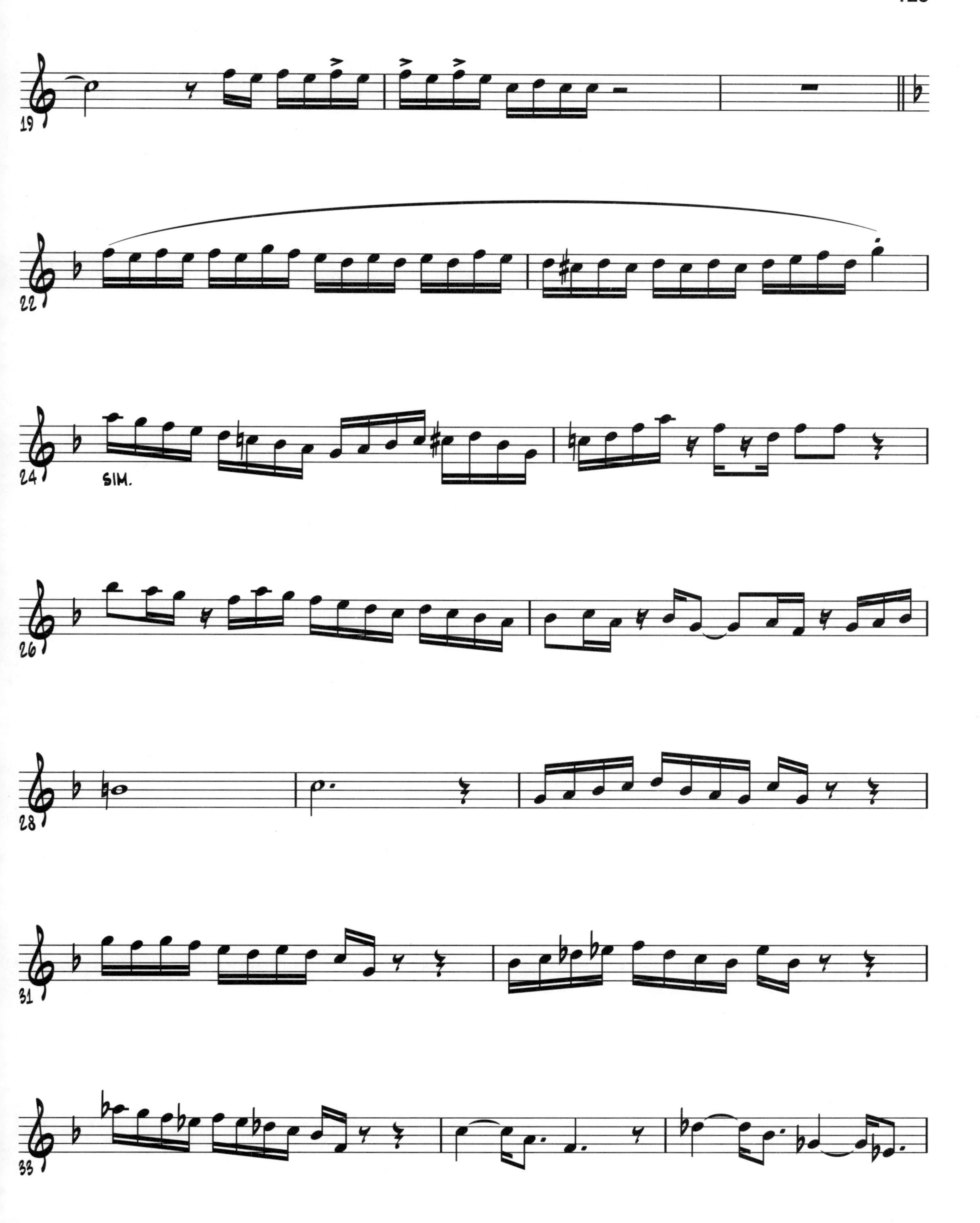
19
22
24
SIM.
26
28
31
33

36
39
41
43
46
48
50
53

JAZZ ETUDE 64

mf
p
ff
mf
mf
mf
EVEN 8THS
p
ff

67
70
mf
73
76
79
f
84
mf
87
90
mf
94
97

100
f
104
mf
mf
107
110
113
116
f
119
mf
122
fff
f
126
cresc.
3
128
ff

Jazz Etude 65

LYRICAL
fff

JAZZ ETUDE 66

JAZZ ETUDE 67

JAZZ ETUDE 68

13
15
18
20
23
26
30
32
35

37
39
41
43
mf
45
47
49
51
53

55
57
60
62
65
69
73
75
77

JAZZ ETUDE 69

JAZZ ETUDE 70

33
mf
SIM.
36
39
42
45
48
51
54
57
60
63

Jazz Etude 71
(A Ballad)

Jazz Etude 72

A REMINDER

LEST WE FORGET:

As promised early on, we are dealing head on with the language of jazz or jazz syntax. For some unknown reason, I prefer the second term. It feels a bit more friendly to me. In fact, we are dealing with its most salient feature: MELODY.

By now, you have played or practiced from this method book many jazz melodies, so that hopefully, you are beginning to "melodize" your general mindset. When a jazz player is improvising, he is composing on the fly but in real time, melodizing on the fly in real time.

Here in the new millenium, I can only hope and pray that you band directors, music teachers, (all age levels), grade school, high school, and colleges will expose children to the world of jazz at a much earlier age level than is customary. On the other hand, I am keenly aware of the fact that some progress is already taking place in some locales. That is a very good thing. Also, some jazz institutions are far more forward thinking than others.

At this point, I would like to briefly cover just a few other areas.

I personally have not explored multiphonics (playing more than one note at a time), or circular breathing, which really sound intriguing as well as functional. I strongly urge you to investigate, because the practitioners get outstanding results from both.

My personal practicing routine? I thought that you would never ask! :-)

This is a general practice routine that is not etched in marble. This practice routine was used while I was still touring and performing live.

It also mainly applies for the so-called dry spells in between "gigs" or performances. When you are performing on a nightly or regular basis, you don't have to or need to maintain such a militaristic approach except for the discipline it imposes, which just may be good for you as it was for me.

The start of the practice routine is to do long tones, not very loud, usually until the breath expires. Next are scales, about a mezzo-forte, first at a moderate speed, then increasing in pace. These start at a low E below the staff to high F and back down.

(Refer to the exercises in this book: "Start To Move Around" (page 29), and "More Move Around" (page 30), in Part One of this book.)

At this time, I take a break, then more long tones, this time at random, unpredictable intervals with a sforzando attack followed by a soft sustain. Mixed in with this are triadic patterns. Then, I play staccato octave jumps over three or four octaves up and down.

Then, lip glissandi, very random and wide ranging.

Then, a ballad standard (maybe two or three) and/or free loose, rubato improv on 12-bar blues, any tempo and any key. Next, I will again articulate cyclical but rambling patterns based on any and all chords.

At this point, things become even more random and more unpredictable, in all registers.

(Many of the etudes in this book are based on fragments or motifs that I created while noodling around or practicing.)

After that, I will have no more practice until approximately bedtime. Before going to bed I improvise with "play along" CDs, for 30 to 45 minutes.

Oh, what fun, because with no audience I take more chances. I am more adventurous and do a bit more of living on the edge.

You may ask: J.J., since you are retired, why do you continue to practice? A very good question, indeed. My reply? Because it feels so very uncomfortable NOT to practice. Old habits never retire. :-)

Also, I enjoy practicing. I get an added bonus: It's another form of physical and mental fitness.

In summary, practicing should be a joy and a pleasure, so do try to stay focused, but in a loose, relaxed mode. Also, try to acquire and maintain the melodic mindset.

The legendary music teacher and genius, Arnold Jacobs, had this to say: "Skill is developed over a period of time in spite of yourself."

In Conclusion

The New Millennium! What an exciting time to be involved in the arts, and especially to be involved in jazz music. The future looks bright and promising.

I am encouraged when I listen to jazz recordings that are being released by the recording companies, even though the feverish pace in which the releases come to us sometimes borders on overkill. Cutting-edge technology is also involved in the process used by recording companies, and that is a good thing of course. Again, the future promises.

Other new jazz method books will also be forthcoming in the new millennium, and that too is a good thing.

Nothing could ever give me more pure joy and personal satisfaction than to learn that THIS method book has made some small contribution towards bringing us even closer together as TRUE KINDRED SPIRITS.

Yours truly and sincerely,

J.J. Johnson

BIOGRAPHY

What Charlie Parker was to the alto saxophone, J.J. Johnson was to the trombone. He was the first to translate the new jazz called 'bebop' to the instrument, combining an amazing technical command of the trombone with a harmonic and melodic sensibility that made him an important innovator even as a young man. He was also a talented composer/arranger, writing for small groups and large orchestras with equal skill and great acclaim.

James Louis Johnson was born in Indianapolis in 1924. He took piano lessons as a child, and first picked up a trombone at the age of fourteen. His influences were Vic Dickenson and particularly Fred Beckett, soloist with Harlan Leonard and His Rockets. Primarily self-taught, he played in the territory bands of Clarence Love and Snookum Russell while still in his teens. His first big break came when the Benny Carter orchestra came into town to play a theatre date and a trombonist was needed. Johnson played with the band, and Carter immediately hired him, first asking his family's permission. Johnson stayed with the band for three years, recording his first solo on Carter's Capitol Record "Love for Sale," (1943), and composing and arranging for the band as well. Johnson also participated in an early Jazz At the Philharmonic concert in Los Angeles, with Nat "King" Cole, Les Paul, and Illinois Jacquet.

Johnson joined the Count Basie band in 1945, but by 1946, he was in the forefront of the modern jazz world as a soloist and leader of groups. He worked with Parker, Dizzy Gillespie, Bud Powell, Fats Navarro, Miles Davis, and a young Sonny Rollins. However, by the early fifties, he'd left music to be a blueprint inspector.

In 1954, he and trombonist Kai Winding put together a group called Jay and Kai (Kai pronounced his name "Kay" during that period). The quintet was quite popular and made some spectacular recordings, but work was not as plentiful as it should have been given the talent of these two men; because of the racial makeup of one black and one white leader, touring and hotel accommodations were still problematic in the 1950s. Each formed his own group by 1957, although Jay and Kai did get back together for occasional tours.

In 1956, J.J.'s "Poem For Brass" showed his immense talent as a composer of concert music, and such pieces as "El Camino Real," "Sketch for Trombone and Band," and "Perceptions" were commissioned and recorded. In 1970, J.J. went to Hollywood to write and orchestrate film and television music, and for a number of years virtually retired as a trombone player.

However, by the eighties, he returned to active playing and toured with trombonist Al Grey, reviving the two-trombone quintet format. He moved back to Indianapolis and eventually retired from playing, but not before he recorded a stunning album for brass orchestra, and appeared as soloist on an album he'd long wanted to make: *Tangence*, arranged and conducted by his favorite composer/arranger, Canadian Robert Farnon.

The book you are now reading was one of Johnson's last projects. Originally a folio for the trombone, the music was too vital and challenging to restrict to 'bone players. J.J. authorized the creation of a treble clef edition soon after the bass clef book completed production. Unfortunately, he was quite ill by that time, and he was in such pain that he withdrew from even his closest friends, finally ending his life on February 4, 2001.

This publication honors his memory.